Thoughts of a Married Woman

The Reflections of My Heart

Lisa Renee
Hutchins

Contents

PLANS

MARRIAGE

TURNING POINTS

DIVORCE

GROWTH

About the Author

Thank You

Inspiration

I am grateful for the opportunities and experiences of being a married woman twice. Marriage can be a union like no other, filled with unconditional love, respect, and support. Marriage provides an opportunity to build a foundation of everlasting memories, love, and the amazing experience of raising children together and passing on your legacy and family values.

I also learned that letting go of a marriage does not define you as a failure or a person who is not enough. People grow up with different experiences, beliefs, family goals and expectations of the meaning of marriage. It is ok to free the family from an unhealthy marriage because all people within the family unit deserve healthy lives and opportunities to grow.

I continue to be inspired by the power of love. I just have to be open to the love designed for me.

Dear Married Women

Many of us spent time as young girls wondering who our husband would be, what our house would look like and how many children we wanted to have. As we grew older, we daydreamed about our fantasy wedding, the beautiful dress, the sparkly ring, the elegant cake, our first dance, and our honeymoon to a tropical island. Our husband would carry us through the white picket fence and into the house we would call home. The house would be filled with the things we built together and the family we made. A place to be loved, cherished, and respected. It all seemed so magical and perfect.

One day, we actually met the man who changed our hearts, and we were overjoyed at the thought of being his wife. He proposed, and we said yes! Even though we may have pushed a few of our reservations aside, we could not wait for our dreams to come true. We embarked on this journey called marriage, and the fairytale began.

We quickly realized that marriage is one of the hardest things we could commit to in life. It came with extreme ups and downs and the realization that we have different expectations about marriage, roles, communication, raising kids, and dealing with each other's families. We learned to grow, adapt, and love what our marriage becomes.

Sometimes, however, our white picket fence gets damaged, filled with fire, and burned to the ground, leaving us with a pile of ashes. This is when we have our turning point. We either find the tools to rebuild our home and repaint the fence to protect it, or walk away because the damage is beyond repair. Whether we choose to stay or leave, we can all relate to the life of a married woman.

New Love

The Timeless Foundation of Friendship

You sat at my desk for hours, days, and months
Watching the tears roll down my face
Listening to my broken heart
Bringing me meals to brighten my day

Teaching me that forgiveness was freedom
Helping me find my smile
Rebuilding my shattered walls of trust
Investing time in uncovering my happiness

Sharing your laughter was food for my soul
Building the foundation for an everlasting friendship

A Special Connection

In life, we meet people every day
Some pass by
And others become acquaintances

Then there are those
With whom we automatically connect
Forming an instant bond

As time passes
We share stories that expose our souls
Jokes are told, laughter is contagious
Enjoying each other becomes a routine

As hard times approach
Support and understanding come naturally
We give advice
Encouraging each other to stay strong

Sacrificing is easy

Because we want to share each other's success

We are open, honest

Keeping the friendship true

A special connection is hard to find

But I found that in you

The Warmth of a Smile

As you watched me walk your way
The sun glistened off my skin
A slight breeze softly blew through my hair

As your warm smile appeared
The butterflies fluttered in my chest
Making my heartbeat soar

As you welcomed me in
The long-awaited embrace was comforting

As you sparked intriguing conversation
The electric connection flourished
Filling the air with currents of laugher and happiness

As we said goodbye
Your embrace soothed my fears
Calmed my ever-flowing emotions

Reminding me of the joy
A warm smile could bring

Magnetic

A man walks into the room
With a sleek, smooth confidence
Smiling with a contagious energy
Dressed in a sexy suit

Standing with a purpose
Suddenly and unexpectedly
He spots the woman of his dreams

She is beautiful, confident, and full of joy
The glow of her aura steals his heart

Slightly intimidated by her presence
He waits patiently for an opportunity

When their eyes meet
The attraction is instant
The laughter is undeniable
The conversation is natural
The connection is magnetic

Igniting the unbreakable destiny
She is going to be his forever

Sangrias

Our Sangrias swirled with fruit and ice
As we casually sipped our drinks
Laughing endlessly

The happiness in my glass
Softly trickled down my throat
Filling my stomach with trust and compassion

The ice cubes began to melt
The more glasses we shared
The warmer your innocent touch became
Never hinting more than a soothing connection

Our evening was coming to an end
As I started to leave
You softly grabbed my hand
Guiding me into your arms

Gently kissing and embarrassing me
We slowly caressed each other
My body yearned for your embrace

I gently straddled you
Holding you close
Massaging your smooth shoulders

You stared into my eyes
Connecting with my soul
The gentle observation of our bodies
Felt genuine and true

As you sat back to watch me
You captured my feelings
Your right hand slowly moved up my chest
Lightly grabbing my neck

Thoughts of a Married Woman

I softly touched your hand, and I leaned back
Your left hand gently rotated my hips
So, I could feel your body between my legs

You ignited me with the desire for your affection
Your patient and caressing touch
Opened my heart

Your body's scent intertwined with my chest
Leaving me mesmerized by your pheromones
The intensity between us was undeniable

As we reluctantly untangled
The sensation of our skin
Irresistibly reconnected
Embracing us with emotions

New Love

We slowly cooled down

Finishing our sangrias

That were streaming beads of sweat

Like your love trickling down the side of my heart

I softly kissed you goodbye

Holding you close

Anticipating the day

We will share Sangrias again

Connection of the Senses

The eyes connect
Capturing the emotions burning inside
With a slight glance
Intertwining an undeniable passion

The ears relax
To a melody that makes the soul flutter
With a soothing sound
Igniting an internal flame

The noses fill
With the scent of attraction
From an enticing aroma
Triggering unforgettable memories

The mouths touch

Overflowing the hearts

With a passionate current of love

Strengthening an embrace that feels like forever

In Your Presence

In your presence
I feel safe

When you smile
It's contagious

When you laugh
It fills me with happiness

When you assist me
I feel appreciative

When you confide in me
I feel close

When you are in my home
It feels right

When you hold me

I feel secure

When you hug me goodbye

I feel like you never truly leave

A Night of Seduction

He quietly opens the bedroom door

He looks to his right

And there she is

Standing in the bathroom doorway

Wearing a short satin turquoise bathrobe

That is slightly draped open

Revealing her sexy lingerie

Her soft blonde hair is curled

Lying over her breasts

The dim light shimmering off of her skin

As her jewelry glistens

Her white stilettos accent her sexy legs

He closes the door with excitement
As she walks towards him
He sits on the edge of the bed
Mesmerized by her beauty
He touches her smooth skin

As the candles slowly burn
The aroma of love fills the air
Their shadows silhouette in the candlelight

She passionately undresses him
Caressing his muscular body

She lays him on the bed
Gently straddles him
Staring into his eyes
She leans forward and begins massaging his neck with her tongue

Thoughts of a Married Woman

As he glides his hands down her back
She moves to his soft lips
Kissing and sucking them passionately

She slithers her tongue down his chest
Kisses around his lower stomach
Then places her mouth around him

With her hand and mouth moving together
He softly moans for more
Moving her hair to get a better view
He yearns for her body

She slowly climbs on top
Gliding down and shifting her hips
She presses her chest against his

Wrapping her arm around his neck
To get a better grip

Softly biting his earlobe

He firmly grabs her ass

As it pounds against him

She softly whispers her desires

He switches positions

Slithers down and latches on

She instantly grabs the pillows

As the touching and licking continue

Her breath gets shorter and louder

He gently unlatches and stands up

Licking his sexy lips

He places her legs over his arms

Slides in gently

Her body instantly feels the pressure

As he leans in holding her tight

Thoughts of a Married Woman

Softly pulling her hair
Telling her how much he loves her
They gaze into each other's eyes
Enjoying the love

Embracing their eternal fire
Reaching ecstasy as one

Glowing

The smile in her eyes
Brings a light she never saw
Showing her a love she never felt
Exuding a feeling everyone desires

Unexpected Love

Unexpectedly
You came into my life
Slowly but surely

Openly
You shared yourself with me
Indirectly but freely

Surprisingly
You genuinely cared about me
Hesitantly but reassuringly

Fortunately
You looked past my scars
Shockingly but nonjudgmentally

Happily
You comforted my mind
Suddenly but consistently

Cautiously
You moved my way
Resistantly but readily

Honestly
You kept your word
Forwardly but respectfully

Confidently
You trusted me
Slowly but surely

Bubbles in the Candlelight

After a lovely romantic dinner out on the town
They start the jets in their hotel room jacuzzi bath

She excuses herself to the bathroom
Slipping off her evening gown to freshen up

She slowly walks out
Into a room filled with candlelight
With their favorite song playing in the background

He stands up in the jacuzzi
With only bubbles trickling down his sexy body
Extending his hand for her to join him

She walks through the red flower petals
Letting her white satin robe slide to the floor

He helps her in
Handing her a glass of pink rosé with raspberries

They sit down in the bubbles
Toasting to the romantic moment
Taking a tiny sip

She gazes into his eyes, wondering what was in store
She slightly turns around to set down her wine glass

As she turns back around
He is holding a box open with a dazzling ring

Her face lights up with joy
As he asks her to be his wife

Saying yes with tears in her eyes
He takes the ring out
Carefully slides it onto her finger

Thoughts of a Married Woman

She holds her hand out to look at it
As the diamonds sparkle in the candlelight

She hugs him ever so tightly
Telling him how much she loves him

He leans against the jacuzzi tub
Holding her in his arms

They look out of the hotel bay window
Gazing at the waterfront
Entangle in the thoughts of their future together

Plans

The One

You wonder your whole life about
Your husband or wife
Who they will be
What they will look like
And what they will do

You wonder when you will find each other
When you are young
When you are old
When you are happy
Or when you are sad

But it's when you stop wondering
They find you
They put you first
Loving you endlessly

They are just what you imagined

The best friend

The lover

The soulmate

You always dreamed of

You know they are the one by

The spiritual connection

The security

The honesty

And the unconditional commitment

The Road Less Traveled

Continuing her adventure to find the right dress
She and her daughter stumble across this hidden wedding store
The sign outside the door says,
"Going Out of Business; Everything Must Go Today"
Something encourages her to just give it a try

She walks into the store with her daughter
There are several brides rummaging through the dresses
All trying to find a beautiful gem in the mist of the madness

Looking through the wedding dresses rack after rack
She feels discouragement inside
Wondering if she will ever find the right one
She faithfully looks one last time

She pulls a ruffly dress back, looking at her watch
Her daughter smiles with excitement, tapping her mother
Time stands still as the elegant satin gown captures her heart
Quickly, she takes it off the rack rushing to a dressing room

It is beautiful
A strapless, ballroom gown with a slimming waist and a bustled train
She spins around in a circle, glowing with confirmation in her eyes

They rush to the counter, happily buying the dress
Jumping for joy

Wedding Plans

Together, we spent months
Searching for the perfect rings

Choosing our wedding colors
Deciding on a location and the menu
Selecting our attendees

Picking our wedding songs and creating playlists
Meeting with the Pastor for counseling
Patiently providing our input on all of the decorations

Participating in multiple rehearsals
Spending time coordinating family travel plans

Getting all the groomsmen fitted
Agreeing to the photoshoots

Making the celebration of us
A day I will never forget

Vows of Intent

As I write my vows

My feelings are moving faster than my pen

As I write my vows

My heart is filled with overwhelming joy

As I write my vows

The struggles of my past stream down my face

As I write my vows

My body is healed from the pain

As I write my vows

I'm ready to love

As I write my vows
I know I will give you my all

As I write my vows
My love is engraved in my words forever

Not Enough for You

As I pack your bag for our wedding day
I hope you see all the love

The time I invested
Making this a union you will always cherish
Showing you the eternal love you deserve

In hopes that all my love is enough
To keep you happy forever

Deep down inside
I know it won't be

As there is a piece of your heart
I can't touch

So, I am going to hold you and love you
As long as you will let me

Making memories that will last forever
Even when we don't

Day Dreaming

As I sit here watching the sunset
I catch myself daydreaming
The new beginning of being your wife

The excitement of styling my hair
Putting on my makeup
Zipping up my satin dress
Slipping into my glass slippers

Wearing my dazzling ring
Smelling my elegant bouquet
Seeing your handsome face
Being the reason for your happiness

Walking down the aisle to you
Touching your hands as we say our vows
Kissing my husband for the first time
And taking pictures that will last a lifetime

Slowly realizing my life was going to change
My daydream was becoming my reality

Farewell

Tonight, I say goodbye
To a place I call home

Taking the leap of faith
To embark on a new journey

Learning how to live a life with another
Building a legacy to remember

Marriage

Is This Forever?

As I stare in the mirror
My reflection looks back at me

I see a beautiful bride
Silky brown hair draping over my shoulder
Tan skin glistening in the light
Makeup showing my radiant glow

An elegant dress that fits perfectly
Jewelry and a ring made for a princess
Roses and peonies filling my bouquet
A smile that I can't erase

My reflection then spoke to my heart
I felt a woman excited to be your wife

A heart that loved your soul
A body that yearned for your touch
A mind that trusted your commitment

But the fear it might not be enough for forever

Warning Signs

She asked God to send her a sign
He heard her crying out
Fiercely delivering one warning sign after another

Her fiancé didn't officially propose
All the rings, cars, and credit cards were in her name
Her wallet supported all the kids

Still ignoring the writing on the wall
She continued forward with the wedding

The day arrived
She was standing in the bathroom
Putting on her final touches
When the phone rang

"Ma'am, do you authorize a purchase for,
$2,000 in rims for a BMW?"
Her heart dropped as she said,
"Absolutely not!"

The red flag to her future waived ever so bright
Feeling suddenly conflicted to call off the wedding

She hid the red flags in her garter
Thinking marriage would hold him accountable
Not wanting to accept the truth

She happily walked down the aisle
Signing up for a death sentence of financial ruin

The Journey to Forever

Off into the sunset they go
Husband and wife

Their smiles are shining
Their hearts are full of love
Honking as they wave goodbye

He gently grabs her hand
Gazing into her eyes
Promising forever

Kissing her softly
Embracing their souls
On their journey to forever

Woven as One

When your heart found mine
It beat alone

The laughter and conversation
Allowed our hearts to touch
Gently with a purpose

As they instantaneously intertwined
They began to beat as one
Weaving together forever

You Healed My Heart

You gently removed the walls around my heart
Layer by layer

You slowly opened the locked doors
One by one

You surrounded my wounds with honesty
Conversation by conversation

You introduced your heart to mine
Minute by minute

You intertwined our souls
Day by day

You restored my heart
Beat by beat

Strength in Commitment

Every couple disagrees
They get hurt, upset, and even cry

But it's how they disagree
That shows their true commitment to love

Their ability to control their tempers
Their willingness to be open-minded

Their understanding to forgive and comfort
Their desire to agree on a manageable solution

Their ability to move forward together
Without looking back

All I See Is You

When we first met
I was intrigued by your voice
My curiosity to learn more ran wild
But my willingness to trust was slim to none

You invested the time to be my friend
Comforting me through my struggles
Quickly becoming the only man
I have ever been able to count on

You always told me the truth
Which I couldn't always handle
But you planted seeds

Allowing me to heal myself
To truly trust a man
By teaching me how to care about the things I could change
And letting go of the things that I couldn't

You became the only father figure to my children
Teaching them to be independent
Investing in themselves
How to respect me as their mother

You have taught me that I can depend on you
Trusting you to wear the pants in our house
Which was very hard for me to relinquish

God has allowed us
To build a foundation
On trust and commitment

Teaching us that
Growing together is easier than standing our grounds
Apologizing is essential to healing our wounds
Investing in us will take patience
And continually improving our relationship takes two

The Illumination of Unity

The moment he saw the bride
She captured his heart

As she was walking down the aisle
His smile was undeniable
She elegantly stood before him

His energy was pure
Ready to receive her love
Exchanging vows with a few laughs
Their bodies filled with joy

He gently took her beautiful hand
Confirming his love

He slid on her sparkling ring
Putting their hearts together
Sharing a first kiss
They became one

Raising their hands in celebration
He stared into her eyes
Confirming this was it

He happily took her hand
Walking down the aisle
As husband and wife

Sharing the journey of happiness
To their unity as one

The Lonely Bride

The sign says "Just Married"
But a beautiful bride drives away
Alone in her wedding dress

Quickly realizing
That she is leaving how she came
Alone

She waits for him to come help her take off her dress
To share that private moment as one
But he never shows

Knowing she would never come first
She hung up her dress
Alone

Feeling second to his family

Understanding her feelings were disregarded

She pulled up her bootstraps

Entering a marriage filled with loneliness

Lunch Time Sounds

She gently opens his office door
Quickly closing it behind her
Greeting her with a smile of surprise

She lays him back on the desk
Sliding on top, swiftly gliding up and down
He caresses her body
As she holds him close

Intensity increases their rhythm
As the sweat trickles down her back
He slowly brings his chest to hers
Embracing her tightly

Their hearts race with excitement
He gently picks her up
Draping her legs over his arms
Carrying her to the wall

While he starts penetrating her body

Trying not to make a sound

The connection ignites

Kissing as they get dressed

She whispers sweet nothings

Secretly knowing

She will surprise him again for lunch next week

Eternally Intertwined

A pair of souls join
Sexual attraction ignites

Eyes caress each other
Hands gently touch
Bodies intertwine

Feelings explore the passion
Creating the friction of love
Perspiration trickles down their bodies

Sounds of desire emerge
Achieving ecstasy

Slowly unraveling
But never completely letting go of the covenant
Bonding their souls forever

Passionate Rewinds

Lingers in the back of my mind
Replaying over and over

Intensifying the temperature of my body
Like a hot sunny day caressing my skin

The uncontrollable desire for your touch
Intertwining the passion of our souls

Weakening my self-control to resist
With the yearning to never let you go

Opposite Shifts

I catch myself daydreaming about you

The glow of your skin
As the sun shines on your face

The contagious feelings
Your electric smile generates

The joyful sounds
Your uncontrollable laughter brings

The soothing touch
Your hands warming my skin confirms

The irresistible smell
Your body shares with mine

The passionate sounds
When we make love

Daydreams
That get stronger every moment
Without you

In His Arms

When he arrives home from work
In the wee hours of the morning
He softly walks up the stairs
Trying not to wake her

He washes off the day
Cleansing with a fresh aroma

She wakes up slightly to the sound of the shower
Turning over onto her side of the bed

He quietly puts on his boxer briefs
Slowly opens the covers
Sliding in, not to wake her with the cool breeze

Gently nestling his body behind hers
Wrapping her with the warmth she was missing

She snuggles into his arms
Drifting back to sleep

Trusting the Unknown

Trust is earned by a partner or a spouse

It is the strength of a relationship

The unknown in trust

Is when they are apart

One may experience

Feelings of doubt and insecurity

While the other

Is confident about their relationship

When they express their feelings

The roles of doubt and insecurity may reverse

Causing the doubtful partner

To take their insecurities too far

While the secure partner

Now doubts the level of trust they shared

When a couple does not resolve these issues

With a clear solution

It could damage the trust and love

They once shared

The Double-Edged Sword

The luxurious side of the sword

Reflects honesty

Revealing hidden emotions

That creates closure

Allowing opportunities for growth

Providing partners with the strength to heal

Building their empire

The dark side of the sword

Creates walls of distrust

Generating feelings of judgment

Uprooting painful, undiscovered flaws

Providing ammunition for relentless disrespect

Stopping partners from bonding

Destroying their kingdom

Turning Points

Keeping Her Blessing

As they sit outside of the clinic
She absorbs verbal blow after blow
From the man that vowed forever

Yelling forcefully in fear
She is overwhelmed with emotions
Her heart is shattered
Devastated by the anger

With tears racing down her cheeks
She quietly asks God to hold her hand

As she decides to give life to the baby girl he promised
She dries her eyes
Shouting her decision
As they drive away in silence

She knows the road ahead will never be the same

Filled with endless thoughts of the struggle

Alone with her children

The only question that remains is....

How soon will she leave?

The Turmoil

One rainy Friday night
The anger of being left alone
Dilated to a three with four children
Overpowered her judgement

As she packed the kids in the car
She drove to the bar
Parked outside of the front door

Kindly sharing her situation with the bouncer
He agreed, out of pity, to let her in
Tightening her long pink bathrobe
She took a breath and opened the door

Swiftly waddling around the tables with fire in her eyes
Searching for her husband
Everyone was staring in shock
Waiting in anticipation

But he had already left
Quickly storming out fuming
She thanked the bouncer
Driving away in embarrassment

She slightly glanced in her rear-view mirror on the way home
Seeing the children playing
Realizing she was the only one in turmoil
Over someone who didn't care

She quickly turned up the music
Encouraging her children to sing along
Masking her heartache

As they arrived home safely
She apologizes to the children for taking them out so late
Tucked them in bed and kissed them good night

With hesitation in her heart
She slowly walked to her room
Turned off her phone and cried herself to sleep

Questions

What initiates temptation?
Is it the situation, the mood, or the individual?

When do you draw the line?
Is it before or after the connection is formed?

Where are you tempted?
Is it at dinner, the club, or being alone?

Why does one stray?
Is it the lust, the unknown, or selfishness?

How do you stop it?
Is it through an argument, a mutual understanding, or silence?

Layer by Layer

When you are upset
You scold me like a child

Your superior perceptions
Clouds the vision of our team

No longer am I the amazing woman
You chose to marry
I am no longer good enough

Attempting to mold me into someone else
Constantly putting me down
Wanting to control me
Fighting relentlessly

In hopes of winning no matter the price

The passion that drives you to be right

Destroys our willingness to understand

Developing a separation

Threatening the unity

We vowed to uphold

The Face of a Liar

Lights up with joy
As you believe their lip service

Frowns in anger
As you untangle their lies

Smiles in happiness
As you trust them again

Freezes with irritation
As you call their game

Yelling with fury
As you are faulted for their dishonesty

Your Spirit Breeds

The intense rush of fear
The flame of anger

The break of the heart
The loss of control

The tears of pain
The sight of denial

The sound of betrayal
The touch of confusion

The words of dishonesty
The false happiness of forgiveness

The Beautiful Waterfall of Flames

Our souls joined, filling our hearts with love
Calming our doubts and fears as we flowed together
Forming a luxurious current of unity

I felt my heart opening to receive your affection
Trusting you enough to share my thoughts, dreams, and fears

Then suddenly, I started drowning
Caught in your undertow of deception

Revealing your aggressive currents of anger
Attacking my character
Attempting to enforce expectations you couldn't maintain

The water quickly turned red
As your disregard for my life spewed like fire
Burning my skin, flame by flame
Numbing my body to the pain
Creating heated waves of devastation
Destroying the heart, you vowed to love

I finally made it to the surface
Struggling to stay afloat

The fire from your yelling was sweltering
I desperately pleaded for your water to soothe me
Before the backdraft of my damaged heart disintegrates yours

As the anger overwhelms my body
I attempt to control the anxiety

Thoughts of a Married Woman

As I could see what was ahead

Swiftly watching your current take me over the edge

I quickly hit bottom and floated to the shore

Still not ready to leave our currents of love behind

I looked around

Only to see you at the top of our burning waterfall

Smiling with a glass of water for one

Realizing I would continue to get scarred by your flames

Until I put out the fire myself

Spewing Destruction

When are you going to stop?
Maybe when I go into a shell,
or maybe when we take a break.

What causes you to use damaging words?
Maybe to shut me up,
or maybe it empowers you.

What makes you want to run?
Maybe to get out of the situation to reflect,
or maybe it's easier than making a change.

What makes you come back?
Maybe you really love me,
or maybe you don't want me with anyone else.

Boundaries

Pictures of a co-worker's personal adventures
Keep coming to his phone
When she thinks the wife is asleep

The FaceTimes from Vegas
When she thinks the wife is not home

The sound of her voice at work functions
Triggers the feelings of a secret competition
When she thinks the wife cares enough to fight for her husband

But what she didn't realize
Was that she already won

The love in the wife's heart was shattered
Knowing his defensiveness spoke volumes

The trust of commitment was evaporated
Knowing he would always keep things a secret

The unity of marriage was broken
Knowing he would never establish boundaries

Dirty Laundry

I lay here smelling like your dirty laundry
The smell of your lies
Lingers in my bed

The thoughts of your deception
Piles up on my heart

My voice of utter devastation
Tumbles viciously through the phone

The sound of your silence
Screams confirmation
You folded someone else's laundry

The lack of respect for honesty
Flooding my mind with unerasable images

The permission you took but didn't give me
Piles to higher heights
Tipping my strength to forgive

That smelly laundry of your deception
Lingers in my tumbling damaged heart

Truth

What is Truth?

A Choice

The whole truth can be revealed,

or just enough to cover the hidden scandal.

Why is the truth revealed?

Freedom

The release of a guilty conscious,

or exposing a mistake that encourages healing.

When should the truth be told?

Always

The secret may constantly distract one's focus,

or potentially destroy a marriage.

Where should the truth be exposed?

Anywhere

The privacy of one's home,

or in front of millions of people.

How is truth told?

Honestly

The sincerity in a confessional conversation,

or a revealing letter that encourages a response.

Disconnected Hearts

When things are good
Your heart is connected to mine

Your face lights up
When I smile

Your emotions embrace mine
When I touch you

Your soul is clear
Because you let me in

But when things get tough
Your heart is disconnected from mine

Your face is emotionless
When I cry

Your expressions of irritation separate our connection
When I need reassurance

Your body is cold
Because your soul pushes me away

The Pain Behind the Ring

The brilliant glistening of the diamonds
Blinds other women
To the pain hidden underneath

The elegance of the design
Masks the weight
To the unbearable loneliness

The clarity of the cut
Mirrors a false perception
To the lack of love it brings

The removal from her finger
Release the anxiety
To the unhappiness it symbolizes

Caught in the Middle

Do you stay for the family?

Denying the need for a true relationship
Risking maintaining an unhealthy environment

Do you leave?

For the positive potential of the unknown
Finding that family bond that breeds positivity

Either choice will ignite an internal struggle.

But at the end of the day
Choose what is best for the children
They deserve the chance to thrive in a healthy home

Unspoken Confirmation

Something woke her up out of a dead sleep
She looks at the clock
Only to discover he is late

With an unsettling feeling in her heart
She checks the family tracker on her phone
Only to see he is in a strange neighborhood

Confirming her worst thoughts were true
She puts her phone down
Only to accept the fact she has to move on

Divorce

Just an Image

On the outside looking in
The perception is perfection

The beautiful couple
The dreamy house
The luxury cars
And the happy children

After taking a moment to peek inside the window
The view is brought to life

The lonely wife
The unkept home
The mounting expenses
And the emotional disconnect with their children

Only for them all to smile for the camera

In hopes of capturing a moment

Where life appears to portray a sense of perfection others envy

One snapshot at a time

Spades of Life

Preying on a naïve woman

Seems like an easy win

Using marriage to mask his hidden agenda

Becoming a superficial team player

As they start winning together

He is secretly using her as the backbone

To support a family

He never wanted

He cuts the suit

As soon as they started losing

Realizing their marriage was not forever

She quickly shuffles the cards

Starting another game

He secretly talks over the table

Not knowing he was teaching her everything

How to survive in a world without him

Finally, she flings her last spade

Across the deck of divorce

The Raging Papers

A man strolls up to his front door
In confusion why his key doesn't work
He notices his clothes in bags on the porch

He timidly knocks on the door
Knowing this is not a good sign
After he was gone and unresponsive all weekend

His wife unlocks the door
Inviting him to the table
As he stands there, analyzing the situation
She begins explaining all the papers before him

The dissolution of marriage
The separation of debts
The parenting plan options

His eyes glaze over in disbelief
Calmly trying to back out
She sternly demands his signature over and over

Refusing to end this
He calmly walks out of the door
Putting his bags in his car

As the tears stream swiftly down her face
She yells in anger for his signature

He ignores her request
Gets into his car and drives away forever

Throwing in the Towel

I wanted to be
The one

To brighten your spirits
Shower you with love
Heal your conflicted heart
Repair your soul
Maintain the life we were building

But my heart slowly begins to break
Knowing I am not your solution

Your internal battles with the bonds
Pulling you back home

The life you are trying to live here for me
Doesn't bring you peace

The strength swells in my soul
As I reluctantly throw in the towel
To give you the freedom you yearn

Knowing one day
It will break your heart
Realizing I will never be yours again

I will always keep you close
But far enough away
From the heart that you broke

Closing the Door

As I walk through our empty house
One last time

I wish we could have enjoyed the view
One more night

The walls were bare
As each memory was removed
Picture by picture

The sound of silence filled the rooms
As our family's laughter was gone
Joke after joke

The presence of our unity was missing
As the fireplace blew out our conversations
Flame by flame

I knew this was the end for us
As the emptiness remained
Moment by moment

I quickly left you a note on the counter
Wishing you the best in life
One last time

You Thought

You thought I would take your disrespect
The lies, betrayal, verbal and physical abuse

You thought my threats were empty
The packing of your stuff
Removing my ring
Yelling I was done

You thought I would let you control me
Verbally, emotionally, and physically

You thought I was insecure
Knowing you had nothing
But the clothes on your back

You thought I wouldn't leave you
Not trusting my independence
Self-worth and need for happiness

No Words

No words can describe the betrayal

Just feelings of regret

Streaming down her face

Silently justifying her reasons for staying so long

Just reminds her of the never-ending disappointment

Breaking her heart by the minute

Walking away in silence

Just seems easier

Praying her lessons in life change her path

The Burning Glare of a Stranger

A glare begins burning through my back

As I turn around
I see a lady
Who recognizes me
But I don't know her

Then I see him
My soon-to-be ex-husband
Who just left my house a week ago

While she smiles proudly, spending her money
Our daughter starts calling for her dad
He ignores her excitement and presence

Divorce

As I stand there in shock
My blood is boiling
My heart is shattered
Our daughter is confused

I quickly distract her
As they check out
Walking away laughing

I stood there, paralyzed
By his complete disregard

For our family
For our daughter

I found a smile to mask my pain
But that glare of a stranger burned my soul

Pride Take a Seat

The rejection letters flood my inbox from employers

As I cash my unemployment check that doesn't cover the bills

The heat from the sun is burning my skin

As I landscape people's yards for extra money

The fumes of the cleaning supplies fill my noise

As I scrub houses from top to bottom

The rude comments fly in my direction

As I leave the food banks in my broken BMW

The glares of annoyance burn through me

As I stand in line applying for medical assistance for my kids

The absence of their fathers and child support restricts me

As I continue to find community resources for help

The pride in providing for my children alone keeps me silent
As I struggle to survive

The constant masking to save face to my kids
As I crumble with devastation inside

The repetitive positive reminders to myself
As I drive through the struggles of life

The determination to show my kids
Everything will be ok

God reminds me
He will not give me more than I can handle

The Backbone of a Soldier

The anxiety swells in my chest
As another day in court comes closer
My hands tremble in fear

Sacrificing endless hours researching
Sleepless nights drowning in paperwork
Uncovering lie after lie
Going head-to-head with a heartless attorney

Endless courtroom charades
As you laugh in my face
Watching me struggle
To raise our daughter alone

Fighting for fairness and justice
Month after month
Year after year
For no reason but

To build a soldier

With a backbone of steel

Ready to fight

Resilient to keep pushing

Through the storms of destruction

No matter how dark the road is ahead

The Man in Her Nightmares

She drifts off to sleep
In hopes of a peaceful night's rest

Suddenly, in the distance
The love of her life appears

With excitement in her heart
She approaches him with open arms
Smiling with the happiness she missed

He invites her to join him at a table set for two
The candle lights twinkling
As he sits down
Suddenly, a red wave of hatred filled his eyes

He places her heart on a plate in front of him

It was bleeding profusely

She sat there in utter shock

As he starts cutting into her heart

Her body gets weak

Filling with anxiety

She begs him to stop

But he slices deeper

Inviting on-lookers to watch

As they laugh with no remorse

He calmly destroys her life

Watching her crumble in despair

She gains the strength to lean forward

Smacking her heart onto the floor

He wrestles her viciously

Trying to regain power

Thoughts of a Married Woman

She wraps a napkin around her heart
But he breaks free
With her heart in hand
Once again

He sits back at the table
Wiping blood from her face

She hesitantly joins him
He removes the napkin
Resuming his destruction
Cutting and cutting

As she watches
This time, she knows what to expect

Her resistance to being controlled by the pain
Slows down her bleeding heart

His desire to bring devastation intensifies
As the on-lookers cheer
Basking in his glory

Her strength for self-worth grows
Teaching her how to ignore the noise
Taking back her power
Owning her soul
Even if she could never take back her heart

Suddenly, she wakes up in a cold sweat
The nightmares of him
Continue to haunt her mind
But no longer control her reality

Even if she knows her heart will always
Bleed a little because of him forever

Chasing Tails

Around and around you go
Chasing one tail after another

Running after the superficial gains
Women can give you

Getting and using
Only to lose the same things
Over and over again

Never keeping what you chased
Because it's not meant for you to have

Only chasing your own tail
Allows you to keep what you deserve

Swirling Tornado

The storm of a broken heart is reckless
Blowing you through life

Losing your purpose and self-worth
Damaging everything in its path

Lacking the tools to manage the storm
Creating dark, thundering, sleepless nights

Dragging days of exhausting sadness
Yearning for direction to calm the fury

Loves Explosive Destruction

Her heart explodes with rage
At the sight of his actions
She sits in the car fuming
Trying to recover from the betrayal

Reacting to her feelings
She jumps out, running around the car
Serving blow after blow
Thinking that was going to heal the pain

Quickly finding herself lying in the street
Waking up angry as ever
Re-approaching him with no solutions

Realizing she is out of control
She quickly gets back into the car
Driving away with her friend, crying hysterically

Searching for answers
Until she looks in the mirror

Understanding she needs to let go
Find the strength to heal

Forgive him for the relentless damage
Learning to control her reactions
Regaining her self-worth
For her own sanity

Misguided Decision

The family in the distant
Opened their doors
Welcoming her broken heart
Extending laughter and memories

One day, a slight stranger noticed her
Offering his friendship
Unexpectedly, he saw her spirit

Planting the seed of deserving happiness
Freeing her from the chains holding her down

The thought of living again emerged
Igniting conversations of crossing unforgivable boundaries
Abandonment making them seem invisible
Trusting the facts solely

She stepped into a new chapter
That was connected to the past

Hurting the ghosts hiding in the wind
Causing turmoil to only be resolved
By honoring the invisible

Sweep Away the Ashes

Trust is like a house
It starts with a foundation
From there, the house takes form
Building quickly or slow and steady

When the house is constantly mistreated
Unwanted frail walls replace the structure
Slowly sparking a vicious flame of distrust

Eventually igniting a raging fire
That continues to swarm throughout the house
Quickly engulfing and disintegrating the trust
Leaving nothing but ashes

The only way to restore the foundation
Is a new house

The Cure

The sound of your voice
Triggers my scars of years without closure

The trembling of your brokenness
Reminds me of a person I once was

As your tears roll down your checks
Your heart overflows with sadness
Showing me that it was my turn to help you heal

The reassurance of my spirit in you
Slowly starts mending your scars

Thoughts of a Married Woman

Encouraging you to open the doors
Cleaning out the devastation of loss
Learning to close the gaps
Creating boundaries for healing

Teaching me that your happiness
Was closure only I can give

Growth

Singlehood

A time for heartache
Fostering sleepless nights of endless questioning

A time for frustration
Holding onto sadness and self-doubt

A time for emotional overload
Denying your desires for your soul tie

A time for reflection
Accepting your shortcomings

A time for healing
Encouraging closure

A time for forgiveness
Absorbing your lessons learned

A time for acceptance
Knowing you can only change yourself

A time for family
Holding your children a little closer

A time for discussion
Creating a safe place to share feeling

A time for guidance
Seeking support outside the box

A time for celebration
Exploring newfound freedoms

A time for setting goals
Motivating success

Thoughts of a Married Woman

A time for mingling
Building genuine friendships

A time for setting boundaries
Staying true to your expectations

A time for patience
Waiting for the right blessing

A time for commitment
Loving an eternal partner

A Woman

What allows a woman to trust again?
Affection, love, togetherness

What keeps a woman believing someone was made for her?
Faith, patience, trust

What keeps a woman single?
Expectations, boundaries, happiness

What sparks a woman to commit?
Honesty, consistency, dedication

What keeps a woman?
Reliability, trust, growth

The Light at the End of the Tunnel

The tunnel looked dark
As it stared her in the face

The tunnel was cold
Appearing endless
As she drove into it for the first time

It was overwhelming
As she navigated hesitantly

The tunnel made unexpected turns
As she gripped the steering wheel, holding on tight

The darkness of the tunnel tried to slow her down
As her vision was clouded

The tunnel gradually became straighter

As she learned how to steer

The tunnel became brighter

As she continued to press forward

The tunnel finally ended

As she drove into the light

Her stepchildren stood there smiling

Making the light

At the end of the tunnel

Worth the journey

Healing a Scarred Heart

The heart is relentless
Experiencing blow after blow
Heartbreak after heartbreak
Creating scar after scar

The heart is strong
Healing the damage after destruction
Year after year
Building wall after wall

The heart is forgiving
Trusting person after person
Time after time
Accepting disappointment after disappointment

The heart is resilient
Moving from victim to survivor
Day after day
Learning lesson after lesson

Erase the Stigma

Refuse to be labeled
As less than

Hold your head high
Look towards the sky

Thankful you chose life
The happiness of peace

Honoring the freedom to fly
Growing your spirit

Fulfilling a destiny
Designing only for you

Soulful Melodies

Creating a magical getaway

Developing fantasies

Satisfing desires

Building connections

Speaking our truth

Drawing endless emotions

Joining bodies

Cleansing souls

Telling a story

Reminiscing

The music brings a smile to my face
Laughter to my heart

Reminding me of positive memories
From the path we shared

Reminiscing with the kids
Making it safe to talk about the past
Laughing about old times

Even without your presence
The kids and I will share those memories forever

Family Ties

Branding family ties

Starts with parents

Raising children together

Building irreplaceable memories

One knot in the rope at a time

Late night sing-offs

Barbeques with family and friends

Holiday shopping for the kids

The laughter shared as one

Strengthens the rope

Creating family ties for life

No matter the distance

God's Choice

God has someone for everyone
He knows who is good for you
And who is not

He will give you the freedom to choose someone
However, if they are not the right one
The relationship will fail

You can pray about it
But God only blesses you if you obey

He will allow you to be loved
All you have to do is listen

Success

Challenges the mind

Encourages growth

Changes perspectives

Tests priorities

Teaches flexibility

Demands focus

Removes distraction

Requires sacrifice

Motivates endless dedication

Breeds goal setting

Accomplishing success

About the Author

I was born in 1979 in Tacoma, Washington and was raised by my parents along with my older sister. After high school, I attended the University of Washington in Seattle. In my senior year, I became pregnant with my son. He was four months old when I graduated with a Bachelor of Arts Degree in Sociology and Speech Communications in 2001.

After graduation, I was a single mother for many years until I married in 2007. A year later, my daughter was born in 2008. I was laid off in the spring of 2009, got divorced in 2010, and struggled on unemployment for a year and a half.

In 2011, I became the Activities Coordinator for the Warrior Transition Battalion on Joint Base Lewis-McChord, helping soldiers rehabilitate. I pursued my interests in project management, receiving my Certified Associate in Project Management in 2014, which helped me become a Program Coordinator, where I helped develop an Education and Training Program. During this time, I remarried in 2016, divorcing again in 2018.

Experiencing this journey of marriage and divorce, I want to share my experiences with other married women to let them know they are not alone. Marriage can be a blessing that shapes us into amazing people. It can also cause a lot of damage over time. Self-love is most important, so always take a moment to recharge, reflect and move on if that is what is required to be emotionally and mentally healthy. I found peace through self-reflection, laughter, and acceptance, which has helped me maintain the love in my family.

Thank You

Thank you for spending your time in my thoughts.
I would love to hear from you.

Connect with me on social media.
Instagram@Thoughtsoflisarenee

LinkedIn, Facebook, and TikTok at:
Author Lisa Renee Hutchins

YouTube at:
Thoughts of Lisa Renee Hutchins – Author

Email me your thoughts at Gmail.
thoughtsoflisarenee@gmail.com

www.authorlisareneehutchins.com

Stay amazing, and don't let your past define you!
It is only a lesson learned on your journey to greatness!

www.ingramcontent.com/pod-product-compliance
Lightning Source LLC
Chambersburg PA
CBHW070808100426
42742CB00012B/2298